I0109079

ROYAL4 PUBLISHING PRESENTS

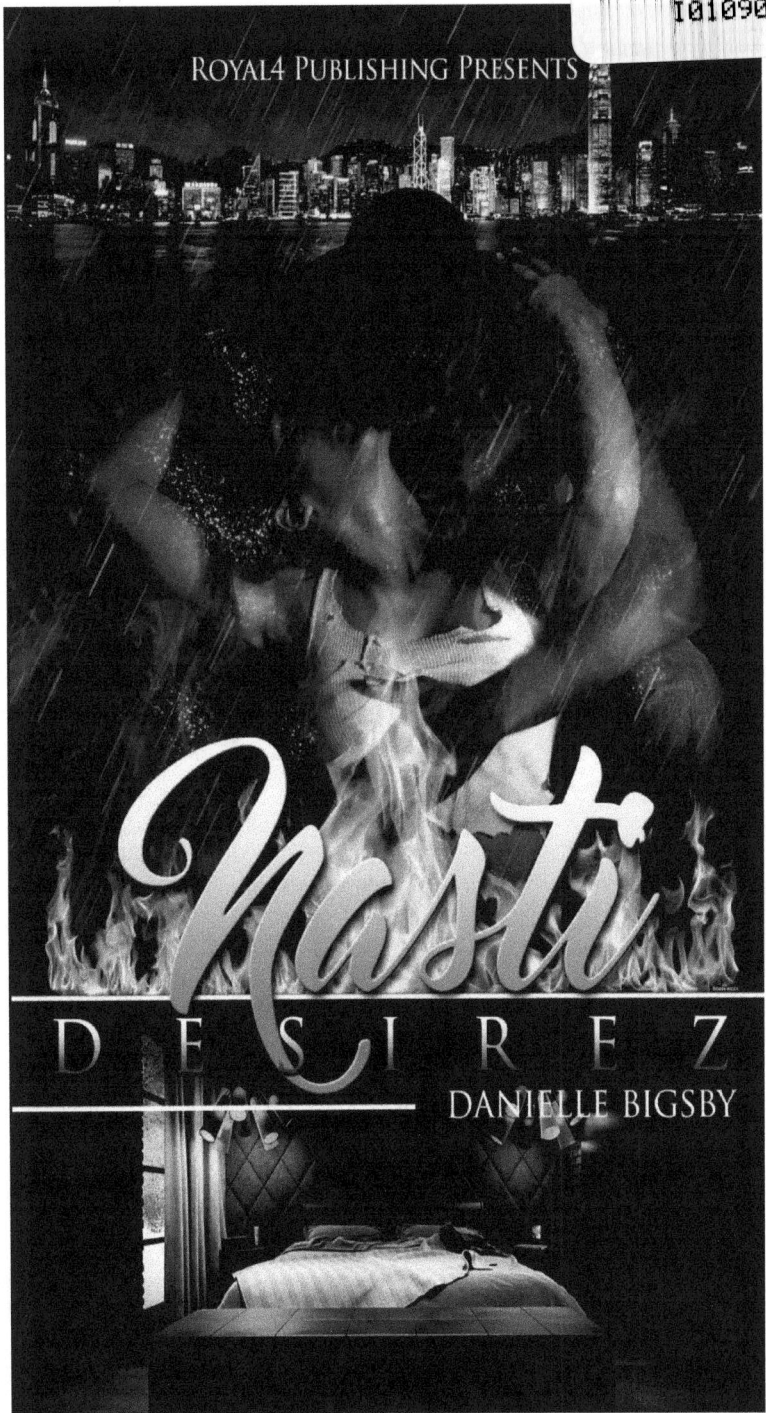

Nasti

DESIREZ

DANIELLE BIGSBY

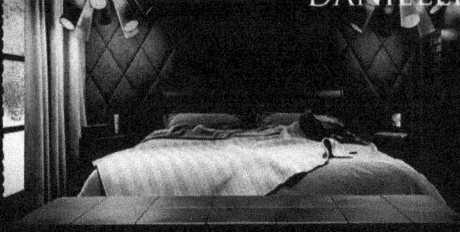

Nasti Desirez

Written by:
Danielle Bigsby

Royal4PublishingPresents

Copyright © 2016 by Danielle Bigsby

All rights reserved. No part of this publication may be reproduced, distributed, or transmitted in any form or by any means, including photocopying, recording, or other electronic or mechanical methods, without the prior written permission of the publisher, except in the case of brief quotations embodied in critical reviews and certain other noncommercial uses permitted by copyright law.

Ordering Information:
Quantity sales: Special discounts are available on quantity purchases by corporations, associations, and others. Orders can also be shipped to prisons and penal facilities at discounted rates.

All our books can be found at the following locations:

Createspace.com

Amazon.com

Queen City Bullies.com

Urban Moon Books: The Indie Author Outlet (Chesapeake, VA)

Maleah Solange Independent Book Sellers (Indianapolis, IN)

Royal4PublishingPresents@gmail.com

Website coming soon!!!!

<u>Dedication</u>

For every woman that has ever felt caged in…

For every woman who hid her freaky side because she was afraid of what everyone (society) would think…

For every relationship that has lost its' spice…

I challenge you to embrace your Nasti Desirez!!!

<u>ACKNOWLEDGEMENTS</u>

Many of us have often hidden our sexual side from others because we were afraid to be labeled as a freak, a thot, or a hoe. Yet refusing to embrace our natural freakiness has caused many of us to become sheltered and afraid to give our mates/partners the utmost sexual experience. In *Nasti Desirez*, you are encouraged to embrace those freaky fantasies and wildest desires…

No journey is as good or feels anywhere near complete if gratitude is not given to those who helped make it possible. I am forever grateful to everyone who contributed in any way to allow my dream to unfold. Whether it be giving advice, listening to me complain, or allowing me to bounce an idea off of you; I truly appreciate it all.

First off: All praises to God. For without His love, mercy, and guidance, none of this would be possible.

Secondly, I want thank my motivating factors: To my four children: **Eniyah**, **Te'Ontez**, **Danterryia**, and **Da'Nae**, I want thank God for placing you in my life. Being your mother has blessed me in so many ways. You have pushed me to chase after my dreams, not just to provide a future for you, but also for my own self-fulfillment. I am thankful and truly humbled to be your mother. I love each of you with all my heart.

Next up, to all those who believed in me when I didn't believe in myself: I truly want to thank you from the bottom of my heart. Your love and encouragement has pushed me to go after what I really want in life.

To all my ex-lovers: I want to thank you for the experiences that we shared. Each of them taught me something different and I appreciate it. Now don't feel too important, because you didn't make me who I am. You just showed me that there were uncharted waters and unexplored territory. Oh trust me when I say I have found that sexual beast that was buried deep inside and she is getting bolder. So thanks for the little parts that you did play. (ha-ha)

Also to the church folks who may feel the need to judge me: Do I love God? Oh yes I do. Without Him none of this would be possible. Am I writing about sex? Yes, I am. Do I promote fornication? Of course not. But we are all human and have engaged in sexual activity at some point in our lives. How many of you have had kids out of wedlock? I'll wait… The bible says, **"Judge not, lest you be judged."** And I will leave you with this, when you are judging and pointing the finger at me, remember that there are three fingers and a thumb pointing back at you. That means, clean out your own closet before you worry about what's in mine!

And finally, to all my sexually free people out there: Let me first say, always protect yourself. I personally have decided to wait on my husband but that doesn't mean that is the right choice for everyone. And to the women who have been sheltered about showing their freaky side with your husband I will give you something that was given to me: **"Don't take Prissy Priscilla into your bedroom with your husband. You better bring out Freaky Freda!"** And to the single women: **your jewels aren't for everyone. Be discreet in who you choose to get nasty with.**

Last but definitely not least: To all those who laughed at me, called me ugly, and said I wouldn't be shit: **How do you like me now? (Ha-Ha)**

Table of Contents

<u>69</u>

Man,
Thinking back on the times,
When I was the 6 and you were the 9.

On your face would I grind,
Enjoying full pleasure as my hips did wind.
Taking you in deep,
Letting you touch as far in the back of my throat as you can
reach.

The deeper your tongue goes,
The harder my mouth strokes.
You feeding my face,
And me simply enjoying your sweet taste.

The more I taste the sweet nectar flowing from the tip,
The more I crave every last drip.
Anticipating the moment,
you bless my tongue with your sticky juice,
So stopping at this point,
Is something that I'm not willing to do.

Bouncing my honey pot against your lips,
I feel my climax building,
It's right on the tip.

Faster and faster,
I'm ready to explode,

NASTI DESIREZ

Hold on tight daddy,
and don't let go.

The fire burning from deep within,
As both our climaxes begin.
Eyes rolling back,
As the feeling of joy spreads,
Nothing can compare to this wonderful head.

We reach our peak,
And slowly come down,
Not really sure if we are ready for another round.

Our bodies exhausted,
Our energy well spent,
Faces expressing pure content,
At this moment,
Another round is just not meant.

But until the next time,
I will always hold these thoughts in the back of my mind,
Never forgetting the time,
When you were the 6,
And I,
The 9.

Are You Serious?

Are you serious?
Yes,
I am.
I want to experiment on your body using a few items,
Starting with my mouth and hands.

Are you serious?
Yes,
I am.
I want to spread vanilla icing all over your body with my
tongue,
Not stopping until your hot rod is completely covered,
And you're ready to feed me some.
But what am I referring to?
The icing or that yummy chocolate stick?

Are you serious?
Yes,
I am.
I want to have a little fun with a fruit cup.
Pour the juices all over your love muscle,
Leaving a trail of fruit as I go.
Using my velvet dagger to slurp it up,
Waiting for you to become submissive and beg me to stop.

Are you serious?
Yes,
I am.

I want to use strawberries to stimulate those most intimate
parts,
Squeeze the juice all around your nipples and heat maker,
Then slowly suck it off in three succulent licks.

Are you serious?
Yes,
I am.
Using those same strawberries,
Inserting them deep within,
Spreading my caramel love over each and every one.
Feeding you every last bite,
Lovers can only imagine such a sight.

Are you serious?
Yes,
I am.
Time to get things started,
Ready to mount my pleasure horse,
Needing to feed your face,
Wanting to give those lips some sweet nectar to taste.

Are you serious?
Yes,
I am.
Ready for some oral penetration,
My mouth opens,
As I await the arrival of my chocolate jewel.
Gasping,
As it enters in a royal fashion.

Are you serious?
Yes,
I am.
As you can see,
My velvet purse craves you,
And your cream filled Popsicle definitely desires me.

<u>The Spot</u>

Sit back and imagine those zones that make you hot,
Is it located on the bottom?
Or closer to the top?

Is it your ear lobe?
Is that the spot that causes your mushroom head to swell up
like a globe?

Is it behind your ear?
Does one touch there allow your liquid plug to hear?

Or is it your neck?
Does that area ignite a flame?
If I kissed you there,
Would I be the one to blame?

Would my tongue flickering across your nipple entice you?
Tell me just what this passionate touch would do.

If I licked a trail down your midsection to the top of your
belly button,
Would it turn you on?

My hand caressing your loaded missile to the point of
erection,
Would that send all of your energy and blood flow in the
right direction?

Or is that spot mental?

The visions of these descriptions stimulating your mind,
Will have you patiently waiting for your mate to return
home,
Sex on demand,
No matter the place or time.

Are You Ready

Are you ready to explore your erogenous zones?
But only if you are sure that you're fully grown.

This is not for little girls,
Who are afraid to discover their forbidden spots.
This is for grown women,
Who need ready and willing men in their lives to make
them hot.

You have to explore new horizons,
Navigate through unchartered waters,
Learn some new tricks,
Try a new position,
Create a fantasy that he relives in his dreams.

Are you ready to experience sugar walls contracting?
Visual stimulation causing you to go home and react,
Having your mate wondering just where your head is at?

Are you really ready for your sexual fantasies to come true?

<u>Just A Taste</u>

Just a taste of my love,
And you are sure to be hooked,
This peach drips with juice with every bite,
Your mouth will water with just one look.

All you need is a small sample.
After that,
This love you will repeatedly want to taste,
Consuming everything,
Nothing left to waste.

Juices sweet as the nectar of a tangerine,
Leaving you craving more,
Calling out my name in your dreams.

One itty bitty taste causes you to have vivid imaginations,
Images of you placing your tongue deep within my sugar
fountain,
Anticipating your next fix,
Wanting another hit like a crack fiend.

Just one taste will change your life,
Make you get down on one knee,
Wanting me as your wife.

Don't drink from this fountain if you're not ready to ride,
Because once you ride this wave,
All inhibitions will be thrown to the side.

Proceed with caution,
Take your time,
Because once you go there,
My love will be the nutrients that are required for you to
stay alive.

I Know How It Feels

I know how it feels,
Your body intertwined with mine,
Tongues touching,
Hands rubbing,
Not a moment of wasted time.

I know how it feels,
When you enter me deeply,
Gasping for air,
As nine inches fill me fully.
Holding on for dear life,
Internal cave being stretched in every way,
Neck biting,
Back scratching,
Passion filled moments etched in my face.

I know how it feels,
My climax at its' peak,
The big O building,
Starting at my feet.

I know how it feels to shake and vibrate,
As if my body is experiencing an internal earthquake.
Orgasm after orgasm,
Until our bodies separate.

I know how it feels,
When it's all said and done,

Balling up from violent spasms,
Until my body goes numb.

You quietly sleep,
Pleasure written all over your face,
Our sex session was amazing,
Job well done.

Rollercoaster Ride

A rollercoaster,
Full of curves and thrills,
Ups and downs,
Smiles and tears,
Passion as well as fear.

My sex fits this description oh so well…

Hands caressing my curves as I climb to the top of your
magic ride,
Step in,
Take a seat,
This thrill here can't be beat.

Prepare for a bumpy ride,
This rollercoaster is only in town for one night.

Grab the handle bars better known as the headboard,
Tonight,
I desire to be your personal whore.

This one night has so much in store,
This ride is like none ridden before,
Liquid sparks will ooze from my very core.

Full enjoyment,
As I begin to bounce,
Like a cougar,

NASTI DESIREZ

Daddy I'm ready to pounce.

Up,
Down,
Left and right,
Make sure you're strapped in tight.

Round and round,
Maneuvering these curves,
As I constantly tell you that this kitty is yours.

Highs and lows,
Tonight there's no limit,
To how fast this fast this rollercoaster is willing to go.

Escalating,
So grab right tight on my waist,
Feel the climb as you begin to smile,
Taking these words into your ear,
"Keep your hands, feet, and all other objects out of the aisle."

Laughing as we begin to descend,
Secretly wishing this ride didn't have to end.
But we have no time to waste,
For the end of this ride is drawing near.

On this ride,
You're entitled to a drink,
And juice is definitely what I recommend.

NASTI DESIREZ

Slurp it up fast,
This ride can get crazy,
Can't slow down the pace,
There's no room to be lazy.

I think I will also have a shot,
But I need something creamy and hot.
Quickly swallowing it up,
The climax is seconds away.

Hold on daddy for one last thrill,
Hands up,
Eyes closed,
Waves of pleasure overcome us,
And we scream out in delight,
All we can do is ride until the moment subsides.

The Thrill

The thrill is in your kiss,
Which set of lips will receive this?

The thrill of your sex,
Constantly keeps my lips wet.

The thrill of you penetrating my thoughts,
Keeps me wanting every minute of your time.

The thrill of me reaching my climax,
Makes me want this moment to always last.

The thrill of my legs continually shaking,
Keeps you in my dreams while I am masturbating.

Thinking of your teeth nibbling my clit,
Got my mind gone so bad,
That I can actually feel it.

Devouring my melting pot,
Giving her a tongue lashing,
Refusing to stop.

Invading my walls,
Trying to reach the back of my caramel oven,
In and out,
In and out.

NASTI DESIREZ

Locking my legs on your shoulders,
Placing me against the wall,
Folding my legs over my head,
Lapping as if this is your last meal.

All in,
Face completely covered,
Grinding my hips,
Feeling my love canal about to erupt.

Eyes rolling back,
Mind spiraling out of control,
As my juices begin to flow.
Down my leg into his mouth,
His oral manipulation has me turned out.

Sexual earthquakes all over his face,
He simply smiles and enjoys my taste.
With one final lick upon my clit,
A violent wave hits.

Showers of honey continually spread,
I lean over and whisper in his ear,
"You are the best!"

<u>Fantasy</u>

What's your fantasy?
Mine includes you.
With your body,
There are so many things I want to do.

Would you like for me to suck you with ice?
I'm sure that would feel nice.

Would you like if I ate a fruit cup off your magic stick?
Slurping up the juices with every lick?

Would you like if I spread vanilla icing from your chest to
your balls?
Licking it off while sliding my breast over your chest,
And massaging them with my jaws?

Would you enjoy me squeezing juices from strawberries
into my love box?
Then feeding you long and slow,
Or would you just prefer my juices to drink on the go?

Would it be better if I sit my caramel oven on your chest?
And dip strawberries inside to give you a taste of the best?

How about a little role play?
High heels,
Fishnet stockings,
Boy shorts and no bra?

Or would I make your day in some sexy lingerie?

Bent over and ass up,
Or legs on your shoulders?

Love making,
Or drilling my juice box over and over?

Face in the pillow,
Or face in your lap?

Which one suits you best?
Fuck it,
I will do it all with no regrets.

Whatever you like is my demand,
If I could,
I would even try a headstand.

Fantasy or reality,
Take your pick,
But one thing for sure,
Tonight,
I'm controlling that dick!

<u>Honey</u>

Baby,
Can I be your pooh bear,
And my pussy your honey pot?

Stick your finger inside my sweetness,
Take a lick,
I promise you won't be able to resist.

Spreading creamy, hot, sticky honey all over your face,
Now watch me lick it off,
Oh how I love my taste.

This honey is too sticky and it needs to be stirred up,
Come insert your wooden spoon,
And make it loosen up.

Watch my honey spread slowly across your stick,
Placing some on my fingers just to give you a lick.
But you're not satisfied,
You want my clit.

Opening wide and letting you have your way,
My honey tastes even sweeter today.

Making your tongue work overtime,
Until my honey starts to melt,
And I continually cream until there's no honey left.

<u>Juicy Fruit</u>

Is my fruit a juicy ripe peach waiting to be bit?
Is your fruit a nice hard banana?
Just thinking of the curve,
Causes me to envision your magic stick.

Is my fruit like an apple?
One bite will keep the doctor away.
Is your sex like insulin to a diabetic?
Will I need it just to survive the day?

Does my forbidden fruit remind you of banana pudding?
Creamy and yummy.
Your passionate tool reminds me of a cucumber,
Long and curved,
The spots it can reach are unheard.

Or does our sex combined remind you of a fruit bowl?
Full of mystery and sweetness,
The heights we can reach,
Neither one of us can protest,
For when we combine,
The sex is the best.

The Passage

Take your manhood,
Place it in my throat,
Be careful baby,
Don't make me choke.

Stroke it deep,
Make me use my gag reflex.
Make me swallow as much as I can,
Massage my head gently between your hands.

Now allow me to be myself and get real nasty,
Let me deep throat it,
While staring you in your eyes.
Now switch it up,
Fuck my face,
Feed me dick,
Long and slow,
Guiding your way into the back of my throat.

My throat is even tighter than my love tunnel,
And when I swallow you up,
It gets wet and gushy.

My throat is like a suction cup,
Slowly pulling you deep within,
Over and over again.

Harder and faster,

As it reaches the very back,
I want to feel your blood vessels emerge as it begins to
erupt.

Hot and creamy,
Running down my throat,
Swallowing it all,
Every last drop.
Your body shaking,
But I'm not willing to stop.

Sticking my tongue inside the head,
Massaging your jewels,
As you swell,
I expand my jaws.

I need to taste it just once more,
It tastes so damn good,
I would drink your juice all night,
If only I could.

You were warned before,
My oral exam is no joke,
Because there's no better thing,
Than a trip down this throat.

Dagger

Your tongue is like a dagger stabbing me deep within my
soul,
Every spot on my body it touches,
Causes me to lose control.
Stabbing my love den over and over,
Causing eruptions from within.

Your velvet sword rotates continuously on my pearl,
Creating trembles in my legs,
Butterflies in my stomach,
Rolls of my eyes,
And loads of external pleasure.

With every dip inside my internal being,
My core violently shakes,
Each spasm creates more internal earthquakes.

Folding my legs over my shoulders,
You invade my ass,
Saliva dripping in my hole,
As your tongue penetrates.

Intense screams,
As you drill deeper and deeper,
Searching for my G-spot,
As you await my juicy treasure.

Tongue fucking,

NASTI DESIREZ

Pounding my ass with your pleasure seeker,
As my chocolate eye puckers for you.

My climax is near,
I can't fight it anymore,
The way you eating this ass,
Has me craving the attention of being your personal whore.

Tongue in,
Face buried,
As I beg for more,
Creamy treats slowly drip,
As you rotate between deep strokes and only the tip.

I buck,
Trying to run,
But the way you're devouring me,
Shows that you're having too much fun.

Still I try to resist,
But it's becoming too intense!
You refuse to give in,
Quickly things change,
And you've placed me directly on your face.

No more being nice,
You demand me to ride,
Grind and bounce,
Twerk on your mouth.
Tease that tongue,
It turns you on.

Grab your head,
Slide ass juice all over your nose,
Fuck your face like it's the last time.

Both holes leaking,
There's no turning back,
Only thing left,
Is to squirt from my ass.

It's so close I can taste it,
I'm about to explode!
I can't hold on much longer,
Baby, I'm going to blow.
Gush like a volcano,
Flow like a river,
Drip like a broken faucet,
Indulge in all this pleasure.

Here it comes,
I feel it in my toes,
Rising to my legs,
Creeping closer to my belly,
Inching its' way toward my breasts,
Until I feel it in my heart.
Powerfully back down between my legs,
Pooling in the center,
Just one more lick,
I'll overflow.

With all the strength you possess,

You start at the space between my love box and chocolate
jewel,
Gliding slowly across each crevice,
Until you reach the center.
In one swift motion,
You dive straight in,
As deep as you can go,
All resistance disappears,
And in unison,
My pussy and ass overflow.

Your tongue is a gift,
Its' powers magical,
I can honestly say it's the best,
One thing's for sure,
The way you eat ass,
I'll never be stressed!

Picture Perfect

Pretty and pink,
Soft and gushy,
Nice and wet,
Good and juicy.

Dark on the outside,
Moist on the inside,
This set of lips opens real wide.

Dripping wet,
Ready for your entrance,
Crying out for pleasure,
Puddles rain from my center.

Expanding,
As you push deeper and deeper,
Creaming with every stroke.

Slip,
Slide,
Slip,
Slide,
Goes your heat seeker,
As it buries itself within my walls of paradise.

Mmmmmm,
Yes,
More,

Daddy give me more.

My body is your campus,
Enjoy your tour.
Tickle my clit,
Watch what you create,
Feed me daddy,
Oh how I love my taste.

My eruption is building,
The after effects are greater than any earthquake.

Enough of this position,
Time to switch,
69's my favorite,
I need to feel your love handle quiver with every lick.

Engulfing the head within my throat,
Expanding my mouth like a hot air balloon,
Squeezing and milking,
I need to taste my treat.

Faster and faster,
Saliva flying everywhere,
Don't tap out yet,
Daddy you're almost there.

Fuck my face,
Treat it like my pussy,
It's all yours,
Sweet and juicy.

Balls swelling,
Blood rushing to the tip,
Pulling my hair,
My head pinned in the death grip.

Your cum oozes out,
Coating the back of my throat,
So creamy and warm,
Good and tasty,
Swallowing it all up.

Sorry baby,
But I was thirsty.

Picture perfect moment,
Forever painted in our minds,
Both my pussy and mouth await the next time.

Erotic Yet Exotic

Red rose petals leading from the driveway to the bedroom,
Candles light up the bathroom.
White rose petals floating across warm vanilla scented bath
water,
Massage oils line the vanity,
The words I love you,
Written across the bathroom mirror.

As I enter the bedroom,
Flowers and candles are everywhere,
A smile graces my face,
And I anticipate all the ways that you will be repaid.

I undress as you exit,
Walking to the bathroom,
In the bathtub waiting,
Is where I find you.

You lower me into the water,
I rest between your legs,
Feeling your nature rise,
Begging for some head.

But that must wait,
I need you squeaky clean.
So I scrub every inch of our bodies,
Paying special attention to our desired spots in between.

NASTI DESIREZ

Now that that's out the way,
We can finally begin to play.

Starting with a little tongue wrestling,
Hand touching,
Finger sucking fun.

Your hands on my breast,
My hands on your dick,
Both of us anxiously awaiting a lick.

My nipple in your mouth,
Nice soft nibbles,
My mouth waters in anticipation,
Your love handle is ready for tasting.

Somehow we have moved from a bath to a shower,
Never missing a beat,
The only thing on our minds,
Is enjoying our special treats.

Standing in the shower,
I drop to my knees,
With a flick of my tongue,
I give the head a tease.

Water rains on my head,
As I swallow you whole,
Switching between strokes,
First fast,
Then slow.

Can't get comfortable,
Time to switch again,
On the wall is where I need your body pinned.

Tonight,
You want to try something new,
So a standing 69 is just what we will do.

My legs on your shoulders,
Your face buried in my thighs,
All I can do is moan,
As your tongue slides inside.

Eating and sucking,
Your strokes feel so good,
I can't utter a word,
Just muffled humming against your dick.

Orgasm building,
You speed up your pace,
And all I can think,
Is how bad I need you to fuck my face.

As I explode on your tongue,
A smile creeps across your face.
You slide out your tongue,
And kiss me so I can have some.
This exchange creates sparks of fire and power,
And as the passion builds,

I begin to devour.
I need you to bust one all in my mouth,
And I can't stop until I have given your dick a full oral
workout.

Finally,
With one last stroke,
And a grunt that can be heard from a mile away,
You release your tasty cum all over my face.

As our session approaches the end,
We smile with joy,
For we are greatly satisfied.
Deep kissing as we exchange I love you's,
This sex session has been long overdue.

Carrying me to bed as I drift to sleep in your arms,
Both my heart and kitty fully spent,
For the best sex comes with no regrets,
And tonight,
You made me feel like a star.

Pure Ecstasy

Our bodies tingle as our tongues begin to mingle,
Lips interlocking,
The passion that is building,
There's no stopping.

Soft caresses and intimate touches,
Fingers molesting,
Walls gushing.

New horizons embark our minds,
Sex is the only option,
Can't waste any time.

Clothes off,
Thrown in a pile,
Needing your sex,
Because tonight,
I want you to go the extra mile.
Every position needs to be tried,
Which way would you prefer for me to ride?

Deeper and deeper,
Real deep between my thighs,
Is the only way I want it tonight!

No soft loving,
Pure hard sex,

The kind that leaves you exhausted without an ounce of
strength left.

Mind blowing,
Legs shaking,
Pussy eating,
Cum tasting,
Kind of night,
No coming up for air,
Until we see signs of daylight!

Pure ecstasy is the only thing on my mind,
So when you're buried knee deep inside,
Fuck me hard,
Bust inside my velvet walls,
And most importantly,
Enjoy the ride!

Anywhere

Images of your body mingling with mine,
The visual has me wanting you,
Any place,
Any time.

Your touch sets my soul on fire,
Every part of your body,
I want to devour.

Your kisses send me in a whirlwind,
They have me secretly wishing,
Our sex sessions would never end.

In the bed,
In the shower,
Or on the couch,
No matter where we are,
Your love turns me out.

Legs constantly shaking,
Load moans,
Headboard slapping,
Leading up to an orgasm that's earth shattering.

Outside,
As the rain begins to fall,
You carrying me over your shoulders,
Your arms wrapped around my waist.

Nothing can contain us,
Only opportunity and space.

In the car,
With the seat reclined all the way back,
Stroking intimate places,
Causing my inner being to react.

Anywhere,
Any time,
Any place,
If the moment arises,
For an orgasm,
All I need is your face.

So whenever your sexual beast awakes,
You pick the time,
And I'll pick the place.

<u>Pearl</u>

Visions of your tongue dancing across my pearl,
Sends my mind into another world.

Up and down,
All around,
Vertical and horizontal,
Circular motions as well,
Licking every inch of her,
Sending me into pure ecstasy.

Kiss her,
Make love to her orally,
Make me say it's the best I've ever had.

Taste her,
Until I push you away,
But don't stop,
No matter what I say.

Continue until my legs quiver with delight,
If you want,
We can stay in this position all night!

Me pulling your hair,
Your tongue going wild,
My pearl beginning to jump,
Damn baby,
I love your style!

Keep going,
Until your tongue causes an overflow.
Wet spots and sticky sheets are next,
My pearl leaks with gratitude,
Anxiously awaiting the next time,
She meets your face!

Sexual Bliss

Just as a seesaw goes up and down,
Our various body parts do the same,
Up,
Down,
Up,
And down,
Sexual favors constantly being exchanged.

69,
Reverse cowgirl,
Doggy style,
Or spooning,
Just to name a few,
Stimulating your mind,
Is what I aim to do.

Wet and wild,
Or down on one knee,
Letting him perform a game of tongue twister,
As he pleasures me.

With a blindfold,
Or with all the lights,
Our sexual encounters go on and on.

Pinned down or tied up,
Maybe using a little ice,
Or some strawberries and chocolate,

Now that sounds real nice.

Each arousing moment brings about sexual bliss,
Sex so good,
Everyone should experience this!

But that won't happen,
I'm too selfish.

Pure joy and relaxation,
Each time we link up,
I can't wait to experience our next round of erotic
stimulation,
Because I simply can't get enough.

His Garden

His garden has nice trimmed grass,
Everything is fresh,
And smells so sweet,
The nectar is so pure,
And the fruit is good enough to eat.

The well is full of water,
And it constantly flows,
Better than smart water,
Such a refreshing and clean taste.
Better than spring water,
Definitely something you won't want to waste.

Smell as fresh as a field of flowers,
With just one whiff,
You can't help but to devour.

This garden is full of exotic pleasures,
One can't help but to search until they find their treasure.

Look high,
Look low,
But leave no stone uncovered,
Do whatever you must,
To cause this secret garden to overflow.

<u>Sex Room</u>

Enter at your own risk,
How strong is your resistance?
Temptation is a mother,
And I aim to make you yearn for this.

In this room,
There are no limits,
Pleasure is your only reason for existence.

No lights,
Only candles to watch the glow,
Of your body flicker in the flame.

Hot oils,
Massage creams,
Handcuffs,
Sex toys,
And a few other things.
This room only exists to complete your fantasy,
And your wildest dreams.

So again I say,
Enter at your own risk,
Because once I'm through with your body,
You will never forget this!

<u>Click</u>

Which pose will you select to make my mental camera
click?

Let's do a photo shoot,
One pose at a time,
The flicker of the camera,
Combined with the silhouette of your body,
Helps me unwind.

Choose one,
Or better yet,
Let's try them all,
Use a little body paint,
And let our bodies decorate the wall.

Paintings,
Drawings,
And portraits.
By the end of the night,
This mental experience,
Will make tonight one of the best nights of my life.

First Encounters

Nervousness fills the room,
As I patiently await his arrival,
Constantly checking my bedroom,
Making sure it's presentable.

Smoothing out my lingerie,
While practicing my sexy walk in my mom's heels.
Trying hard to look appealing,
And trying my best not to fall.

A knock at the door,
My heart begins to pound,
You're here,
All I can do is hope for the best.

My confidence kicks in,
And my walk,
Is one to compete with a runway model,
From this moment on,
Nothing can stop us.

Hands move with a mind of their own,
Lips locking,
With no time in between to breathe.

Clothes disappear in an instant,
Nothing on our minds but getting it in.
Not sure how it actually works,

But we can try what we've heard.

I climb on top,
Trying to be grown,
You kick back,
Trying to relax,
Looking like a deer in headlights.

I try to slide down but it hurts so bad,
I'm thinking to myself,
If only I had known.

I scream out in pain,
And suddenly,
Your expression changed.

We switch position,
And as you slowly glide him in,
You kiss my forehead,
While holding my hand.
Things are much easier,
I can relax again.

Pleasure waves roll across my body and face,
And in this moment,
Is where I forever want to stay.

<u>Ultimate Seduction</u>

High heels,
Lingerie,
Candles lit,
Aroma scents,
They all set the mood,
They get you all in your feelings,
To do things that grownups do.

Sexy body all oiled up,
Ready to be touched,
We've both never wanted anything this much.

Hands on my hips,
Ass poked out,
You lick your lips,
Expressing your taste testing smile.

I anxiously await our sexual session,
Tonight,
I'm ready to learn some new lessons.

To seduce you is my goal,
I want your mind and body together as a whole.

The ultimate seduction would include my body on yours,
Both of us ready to devour,
Grown up seduction going way past the late night hours.

Feenin'

I'm feenin' for your touch,
Longing for your stroke,
Wishing for a taste,
Hoping I don't choke.

Arousing myself while you are away,
Awaiting my climax,
Imagining I was on your face.

Legs quiver and shake,
The tension builds,
Words can't explain how good this feels.

I need you now!
I need you here!
I want so badly to let go of this inner fear.

Masturbating ain't working,
I can't rub it out,
Too many hidden stigmas,
I need your presence,
To work this out.

So come on home,
And join in,
So the feenin can stop,
And real sexing can begin!

Lose Control

Tonight,
Let's lose control,
Be free and wild,
Just completely let go.

Hot, passionate sex is our ultimate goal,
Just what all we will try?
Nobody knows.

In the bed,
On the couch,
On the dresser,
Or on the floor,
My only response is,
"Daddy, give me more."

In the shower,
Or in the car,
My only reply,
"Let's videotape it and become superstars."

Let's get wild,
And hang from the chandelier,
All I want,
Is to feel your body near.

Let's get real freaky,
And cover our bodies in fruit,

Using slow succulent licks,
To drink up all the juice.

Explore new horizons,
And use some sex toys.
One in each hole,
As you devour my clit.

How about a spectator?
Give someone new a view,
Trying to outdo each other,
Who shall win?
Me or you?

Outside at the park,
No shame in our game,
Screaming,
As waves of orgasmic shock overpower us,
Watching,
As others faces become painfully drained.

A little cum drinking,
As you drive full speed on the highway,
The thrill of danger,
Encourages my best performance.

Let's get so wild that we lose our minds,
The only thing that awaits us,
Is time….

What Do You Want More?

Ass up,
Or face down?

What do you want more?

My mouth enveloping your vanilla scented chocolate
candle,
Slowly swallowing every inch,
Cupping you almond shaded tea bags in between my
stiletto nails,
Your hands entangled in my hair,
Guiding my lips further along your length,
Until all 8 ½ inches are covered.

Invading my throat,
Creating moans of pleasure,
Eyes pleading,
For you to give me more.
The look of satisfaction,
Spread across your face,
Gives me the extra motivation,
Needed to complete this race.

Consuming your microphone,
As I speak into the mic,
Loud shrills of thrill echo throughout the room,
My creamy walls erupt resembling waves on the shore,
As your missile shoots to the moon,

NASTI DESIREZ

I quickly drink every drop,
Wishing for more.

Or would you prefer an even tighter hole?

Your rod of pleasure penetrating forbidden territory,
A zone not meant for rough entrances.
My derriere is delicate,
It only opens at your command.
Navigating my onion,
Like it's your own personal strip of land.

Entering slowly,
With just the right amount of force,
Massaging my pearl as you penetrate,
Squeezing my chocolate mounds,
As you drill,
Deeper and deeper,
The moment of ecstasy,
Getting sweeter and sweeter.

A steady rhythm building,
My internal volcano threatening to erupt,
Fingers maneuver around my love button,
As if you are playing the piano,
My ass puckers and blows kisses,
At your well chiseled trophy.
You're fighting it,
I can feel you resist,
Your orgasm is near,
A hurricane is rising.

It erupts like a water hose,
All in and on my backside,
Now that's my idea of honey buns!

What do you want more?
Let me take the choice out it for you,
Everything is possible,
When we do what we do.

I'm willing to try anything,
When we engage in a session,
Every time we connect,
We both learn a lesson!

Bow Down

Get on all fours,
Worship at my feet,
One toe at a time,
Slow licks,
Starting with the pinky toe.

One,
Then two,
Then three,
Then four,
Taking in all your special treats,
But I want more.

A trail of kisses over my entire foot,
Leading up my legs,
Eyes focused on my love dungeon,
But before you taste this,
You're going to have to beg.

Tonight is about domination,
And I am the Queen.
Everything I say,
You must do.

No matter how good it feels,
You are not allowed sexual release.
Defy my rules,
And you will see,

Just how severe the consequences can be.

I am the movie,
And you are the spectator.
You must watch and not touch,
And no matter how hard you get,
You cannot bust!

Your dick cums at my command,
You are powerless,
When you explode,
Is totally up to me.

Sit in the chair,
Hands behind your back,
My handcuffs restrain you,
While I reveal my full body black leather cat suit.

Fishnet stockings,
Six-inch silver thigh high Louboutin heels,
Elbow length fingerless gloves,
Tonight,
I mean business!

No noise,
Just do as you are told,
Remember,
I am the Queen,
And you are my whore.

Disobey,

NASTI DESIREZ

And you will be spanked,
Eyes on me,
And you better not blink!

Pussy so close,
You can feel the heat,
Leg draped over your shoulder,
I shove the tip of my stiletto in your mouth.

"Eyes trained on my pussy,"
"Don't you even think about blinking!"

Watch as my fingers plunge deep inside,
Stirring in circles,
Creating moisture along the way.

Open your mouth,
And out comes your tongue.
Now that was not a part of the plan,
Neither was that what you were told to do!

You were warned,
But you refused to listen,
So things must get kinky.

Stick out your chest,
Perk up your pecks,
It's time,
To get your ass in check!
Gripping your nipples between clamps,
I give them several sharp twists.

You scream out in pleasure,
But again,
You have disobeyed!

Clamps go from your nipples to the tip of your dick,
Twisting with force,
As I give your balls a lick.

Now,
Let's try this again.
Open up wide,
Stick your nose up high.
Nibble on my clit,
As I smother your face,
And you better not come up for air!

Dogging your head,
Devouring your face,
Burying your mouth in between my walls.
Deeper,
Faster,
And you better not stop!

Your dick springs to life,
But my permission was not granted,
You continue to resist,
I see you like discipline.

Hands above your head,
Yes,

I know they are still cuffed!
Lay flat on your stomach,
Spread your body across the floor,
Ass up,
Face down.

Since you love pain,
I will give you some.
No matter what is done,
Under no circumstances are you allowed to cum!

The spike of my heel planted in the center of your back,
Acrylic nails locked in your dreads,
As I yank back your head.
Now watch as I taste my own tits,
Your eyes and attention shall not deviate from this.

But you are hardheaded,
So out comes my secret weapon.
Poke out your ass,
Here comes my paddle.

The spank echoes,
As it connects,
Over and over again.
The sexual tension builds,
But resist your urge to release,
Keep your eyes on me.

Watch as I create my own orgasm,
Resist the desire,

Continue to focus on me.
Watch as I place my butterfly on my clit,
Listen as it vibrates,
Watch my legs shake in delight.
My orgasm is rising,
The end is almost near,
So close I can feel it.

Adding my vibrating dildo,
Fucking myself hard,
About to explode.

Working them both,
My walls begin to collapse,
And my juices overflow.

And as if on cue,
Like you already knew,
You explode.

I'm the Queen,
And you were a good servant,
Now get over here,
And drink all the leftover juices.

Indulge the Freak

For the next 24 hours,
Your body is at my disposal.

I aim to fulfill your wildest fantasies,
To please your innermost desires.
To explore new sexual horizons,
And take your orgasm even higher.

No resistance allowed,
I'm going to search your body,
Like searching through the lost and found.

In search of every pleasure zone,
Every spot that turns you on.
I need your orgasm to reach your inner soul,
But tonight,
You must give up full control.

We can start small to build up your endurance,
But I need you to trust me.
I must have you in your sexiest Victoria's Secret crotch less
lingerie,
In order for me to have my way.

Lay back,
Spread your legs into a perfect V,
Close your eyes,
As I begin to play around inside.

A finger,
Then two,
Then three,
Gliding real deep.

After several moans escape,
My fingers are replaced.
Replaced with my tongue,
As your pearl is manipulated by my thumb.

Start with slow, lust filled licks,
Until my tongue takes a full dip.
Diving in like an experienced swimmer,
While your walls molest the tip.

Sugar cubes melt down your legs from the intense heat,
No release for me,
My only mission is to please.

You have gained some confidence,
And built a little trust,
Now let's take it to another level.

Legs hanging completely over my shoulders,
Basically you are standing on your head,
Ass gracing my face,
As I indulge in my sexual fantasy,
For just a little taste.

Nose, mouth, and all buried deep within,
As your asshole kisses my lips,

Over and over again.

Swallowing every drop of your treasures,
As they escape,
Sampling all your tasty treats.
I could eat your ass all day,
But that would leave this moment incomplete.

So now I must intensify this experience,
Close your eyes,
As I bring out my blindfold,
You must again be willing to submit full control.

A little more taste testing as my hands move within your
hidden walls,
Slipping a pleasure seeker deep inside.
Now stand,
As I place on your new Red Bottom heels.
Hold my hand as I guide you,
Now precede my Queen,
Model for me baby.
Strut like you're on the runway,
With precision,
Walking in a parade.

Get into it,
Twist those hips,
As I watch your sexy body glisten.
Enticed by your moves,
My soldier begins to rise,
Time to raise the stakes a little higher.

I pull out my secret remote,
You're in for a real surprise.
It's been in so long that you didn't even notice,
Nestled between your creamy walls,
Resides a silver bullet.

Your love nest is under my spell,
Can you still strut in those heels?
Only time will tell.

Starting on low,
A vibrating pulse jolts your walls,
And you stagger at the sudden surprise.

Buzzing and thumping,
Vibrating your G-spot,
But you are determined not to stop.

Short, electrifying jolts continue to invade your hidden
secrecies,
Yet you still believe you are ready,
You think you can handle me,
But little did you know,
This heat seeker has ten different speeds!
Increasing the pace,
I watch as pleasure spreads across your face.

Now set to ongoing vibration,
My manhood begins full elevation.
Stroking all nine inches,

In rhythm with your hips.
Increasing speed until the bullet and I are both at full
power,
Your knees begin to buckle,
Then your legs start to shake,
Finally,
Your orgasm threatens to overtake you.
Hold on a little longer I say,
"Daddy wants to cum with you."

You're still blindfolded,
So you can't see,
Just what your performance is doing to me.
Dick so hard,
It could split bricks,
I can no longer resist.

On my knees I go,
Crawling until I meet your waist,
And your forbidden pearl sits upon my face.
Bullet still buried deep,
My tongue flickers across your jewel.

Still stroking my cream filled stick,
Almost to the point of explosion,
Your pearl leaking juice all across my lips,
Our mutual eruption is very near.

Slide your ocean all over my smile,
Allowing my face to drown.
One more stroke is all it will take,

One more twist of my tongue will create,
A mind blowing earthquake.

Trembles in your legs,
Resembling seizures,
Contorting of my body,
Resembling the shakes.
Mutual expressions of pure ecstasy,
You finally surrendered,
And I'm humbled and amazed.

You brought out the freak,
You turned into Ms. Nasty,
Just for me!

Nasty Desires

I am a freak,
And this you know,
When we get together,
Anything goes.

We can do it anywhere,

The bed,
The shower,
The kitchen,
The car.

The park,
The pool,
While going through the carwash.

The roof,
The laundry mat,
Your favorite restaurant.

The dance floor at the club,
The movies,
Or in the Jacuzzi.

On the city bus,
In the limo,
Or at the library on top of the books.

NASTI DESIREZ

At the game under the bleachers,
In the courthouse bathroom,
Or on a plane,
I'm down for anything.

Making a movie,
Or releasing a sex tape,
Our sexual encounters are always great.

Your personal freak,
Slut,
Or whore,
With you I can be my nasty self and so much more….

<u>Lights, Camera, Action</u>

How nasty are you?
For there are levels to this lifestyle.
If your tongue can't explore,
I can't be your personal whore.

I need sex on demand,
Even in public places,
Give the people a show,
As shock waves spread across their face.

We can be the movie that they watch while eating popcorn,
Secretly wishing they could join.
Join in the fun,
And ecstasy displayed on our face.

Some aroused,
Some perplexed,
But our faces only showcase the enjoyment of passion
filled sex.

Each stroke brings more pleasure,
We're in broad daylight,
On the roof of our car,
Without a care in the world.

Another stroke and my orgasm is closer,
And from the look in his eyes,
His climax is also near.

Screaming out in delight as my walls expand and contract,
Against his chocolate love stick.
His hands locked around my waist as he drills me deeper
and deeper anticipating his release.
People standing there with their phones out,
Recording every scene.

Finally,
My back arches,
As my body tingles,
And I release every ounce of my sexual tension.
Your hands lock in my hair,
As your sex stick reaches the depths of my walls,
And my honey and your cream,
Mix together in a sexy cocktail.

We kiss passionately as we turn to our audience and say,
"We hope that you enjoyed the show!"

<u>Lick, Lick, Lick</u>

Trail your tongue across the length of my body,
Taste every crevice,
Enjoy every inch,
As you devour my body piece by piece,
So viciously.

Lick high daddy,
Allow your tongue to snake it's way around to my earlobe.
Slow, succulent nibbles,
Turn into hot, heated, passion filled bites,
As your pink velvet dagger causes an eruption of moisture
and stickiness,
Over and over again.

Travel around to my lips,
Run your luscious tongue across the length of them,
Before diving in,
To taste the sweetness hidden within.

Thunderstorms flood my Vicki Secrets,
As waves of ecstasy crash against my clit.
I'm finding so hard just to endure this,
I can't have him thinking that I'm a little bitch!

Inch down a little lower,
Until your pleasure igniter lands on my neck,
Causing typhoons of enjoyment,

To erupt from that very special hot spot,
As my legs begin to quiver in anticipation of unfulfilled
desires.

Journey on until you embark on the ride of my large and
desirable mounds of flesh,
Implant your hungry kisses on my forbidden fruit tops,
Sending erotic blasts of excitement throughout my body.

Lick a little further south boo,
Crawl down my stomach,
Using your tongue to trail a path of sweet saliva filled S-
shaped licks,
Down to my belly button,
Before dipping in and out to dwell in its' essence.

Travel on towards your destination,
Inhaling my sweet nectar,
Before strategically drizzling soft nibbles along my thighs,
And showering my clit with tongue kisses.

Lick her up,
Lick her down,
Lick her in circles,
Until I can't utter a sound.

Cause my kitty to purr with delight,
As you work your pink magic wand.

Give her orgasmic relief,
With each thrust of your slow churning mixer,

Beating and pulsating my explosive G-Spot,
Time after time.

Creating an earth shattering,
Ear piercing,
Leg shaking,
Pillow biting,
Back scratching,
Hair pulling,
Flood of juices.
Reflecting nothing other than satisfaction and fulfillment.

My body goes limp,
After your session of pleasure.
My smile expresses my gratitude.

Now rest for a short while,
Because in a few minutes,
It will be time for me to lick all over you!

<u>Sticky Indulgences</u>

Taste my treasures,
Enhance my pleasure,
Cause my wetness to drip with excitement.

Stir my caramel oven,
With your stick full of milk,
Creating one hell of a caramel sundae.

Yearn to lick my creaminess,
As it flows down my legs,
Slow,
Sticky,
Sweet,
Just screaming for you to sit and eat!

Come on now daddy,
Sit back and relax,
Allow me to mount your face while you feast.

Your tongue serves as a spoon,
Scooping up this creamy dessert with pleasure,
Lick,
Lick,
Lick,
Lick up every drop.

Stirring up the heat,
Causing your dessert to melt.

Slurping up all of its' stickiness,
Until there's not one ounce left.

One-Eyed Snake

Long,
Full of girth,
Steady and strong,
It's you that I yearn for,
All day long.

Chocolate,
Mouthwatering,
Erotic piece of heaven.
It must run in his family,
And if so,
I want to thank his father for the blessing.

G-Spot reaching,
Pleasure seeking,
Baby maker.
Knows just how to manipulate my body,
Without one ounce of protest.

Creating puddles of love juice,
All over the sheets,
As it penetrates my inner walls,
Oh so deep,
Threatening to take my body to its' highest peak.

Slithering around each sensitive,
Sensual,
Hot spot.

NASTI DESIREZ

Seeking its' prey,
Embarking on forbidden territory,
Until it's ready to attack.

Swelling as its' head launches back in an attempt to
swallow its' kill,
Shooting out ecstasy,
As it indulges in the thrill.

Subduing its' victim,
As its' desires are skillfully fulfilled.
Its' lust for the quest,
Of conquering and devouring has now been met.

The one-eyed python of love,
Has struck once again!

<u>Sensual Seduction</u>

My body,
Standing so seductively in front of you.
Dripping wet,
Exuding sensual scents of tropical passion,
While spreading lingering traces of apple infused romance.

Your body,
Reclining against the headboard,
Granting aromas of temptation,
Yearning to devour my illicit treasures,
As trickles of desire escape your lips,
Leaving trails of fantasies rolling down your cheeks.

Watching my body glisten,
From the beads of water,
Slowly gliding over every crevice of your body,
Pelvis to pelvis,
Feeling the rush,
As your well lubricated chocolate banana split,
Begins to stand at attention,
Anticipating its' turn to bless me,
With a sample of hot, creamy exhilaration.

Your mind has already ejaculated,
At the simple sight of my naked body,
And my body longs to follow.

Pure delight,

Is our ultimate goal,
Because inside these walls of our love dungeon,
Anything goes.

So I beg of you,
Pleasure me.

Pleasure me orally,
Pleasure me mentally,
Pleasure me physically,
Pleasure me seductively.

Cause internal earthquakes,
Provoke intense orgasms,
Allow passion to erupt through my veins,
Release explosive waves through your semen.

My wish is definitely your command,
And my desires are yours to fulfill.
It's something about my body,
It does something to him mentally,
Every time he sees it,
It sensually and seductively captures his mind,
His body,
And his soul.

My fantasies bring him sensual bliss,
And all of my worries,
Are washed away with one stroke of his pleasant love stick.

At Your Command

High heels,
Or stilettos?
Take your pick,
My visual stimulation is aimed at seducing every inch of
your dick.

Lingerie,
Or my birthday suit?
The choice is up to you,
My pussy exudes nothing but passion as my tongue invades
the tip of your manhood,
Enjoying what I love so much to do.

On the bed,
Or on the floor?

In the shower,
Or on the steps?

On the kitchen table,
As I'm served up like a breakfast platter,
Or on the armrest of your favorite lounge chair,
During a football game?

Your third leg causes mental manipulation on each
throbbing nerve of my love nest,
Invigorating my sex drive,
Liberating my inner freak,

Allowing our sexcapades to continue at the highest of
superior levels.

For you,
I'm always willing to be naughty and nasty,
And as long as you continue,
To feed me that good dick,
Nothing is going to stop you from getting as much as you
want of this!

<u>Submit or Regret</u>

Tonight,
I don't want that soft shit,
I want you to yank my head back,
Grip a handful of my hair,
Lock your fingers deeply.

Get rough with me daddy,
I need you to manhandle me tonight,
Force me to take this.

Pin me down,
Bite my neck,
Fuck me so hard,
That I leave teeth impressions and deep scratches all over
your chest.

Place my delectable thighs upon your bulky shoulders,
Require my rosebud to endure the sweet agonizing pleasure
of you giving her a brutal tongue lashing.

Grip my waist,
As you bench press my hips,
While lifting my body weight,
Up and down,
Insisting on bouncing my ass on your tongue.

Rotate my love box wildly against your lips,
Punish me,

NASTI DESIREZ

Stab my kitty with your tongue,
Don't let up,
Even when I scream out in agony and ecstasy.

Penetrate my forbidden fruit with ferocious fury,
Maneuver my love button with the constant flickering of
your pink drill sergeant,
Grant me uninhibited gratification,
Demanding that I relinquish full control.

Recline and watch,
As my body twitches unrelentlessly at your will.
Tonight,
You're the master,
And I'm your slave
Defiance is not tolerated.

Disobedience will cause the erotic torture to continue,
So against my better judgement,
I submit,
And allow you to use my body,
As your personal menu.

Finger Licking Good

Chocolate,
Bow legged,
Dimples,
And hazel shaded eyes.

A go getter in the streets,
And a beast in the sheets.

Luscious, plump, full lips,
He even walks with a dip!
Well chiseled chest,
And a body made to impress.

Just the thought of him,
Causes tingles in my kitty,
Has me biting my bottom lip,
Knowing that he can get it.

Envisioning sinking my teeth into his skin,
As he pummels my kitten,
Over and over again.

Amusement etched all over my face,
Delight oozing from my smile.
Visions causing conflict within my mind,
Wondering if I have enough time,
To pleasure myself,
Because you have me so turned on.

I just can't seem to shake his image,
Layered, oiled, and glistening pecs,
And that six pack,
Damn,
He's blessed!

His body is like a tall drink of ice water,
On a 98-degree day.
It could even be compared to a Pina colada slush,
Easing down my throat,
Pure paradise!

Any tasty treat that one could desire,
Couldn't even begin to compare,
To the wonderful things that his body inspires.

And his penis,
Well,
That too is to be desired.
And on many nights,
Fantasies are what he inspired.

In my dreams,
I swallowed up every piece that I could,
And when he finally released,
It was definitely finger looking good!

I have heard people say,
"Milk does a body good",
But those people,
Clearly haven't met you!

<u>Saddle Up</u>

Most girls are shy,
But I am not,
See,
I have never had a problem getting on top.

You see,
When I'm on the bottom,
I let you do your thing,
But when we switch it up,
Cowgirl takes the reigns.

I boss up,
And take control,
But daddy,
For your sake,
Please hold on tight,
And don't let go!

I'm not your average girl,
I use different tactics,
So in this reclining chair,
Is where I need you to sit.

I don't want to look at you,
I only want to imagine the expressions scrolling across
your face.
Now take both of your hands,
And grip my waist.

NASTI DESIREZ

Don't consider me distant,
If I insert my headphones,
Tonight,
I want to ride you,
Off my favorite song.

Allow me to insert you,
Allow me to glide the smooth head inside my wetness,
I can already feel your excitement,
As you hurriedly pump in and out.
But I have to stop you,
Because tonight,
It's my turn to turn you out!

Pay attention to my body,
As I rotate my buttery thighs,
Feeling the beat,
Vibrating through my clit.

Manipulate my nipples,
Between your fingertips,
Until they ache with desire.

Run your tongue along my shoulder blades,
Softly nibbling into my flesh,
Heightening the mood.

Relish in the moment,
As I place my legs over the armrests of the chair,
And roll my ass cheeks,
Like waves crashing against the beach.

Sink deeper into the pleasure of my sweet walls,
Pulling you in like a vacuum,
Leaving puddles of happiness, stickiness, creaminess, and
contentment,
Each time that they contract.

As the beat speeds up,
So does the rhythm in my hips,
Grinding,
As my clit jumps with excitement,
Aiming to fulfill all your hidden fantasies.

Faster,
And faster,
Until I appear to be twerking.
My hips making love to your joystick,
Igniting an internal combustion.

Juices flowing down my thighs,
My body consistently being slammed against your
manhood,
My hair being held hostage by your fingertips.

Passion flowing from the tips of my toes,
Causing tingling sensations throughout my body,
My climax is near,
My legs begin to shake,
Finally,
My orgasm begins to peak,
And I scream out in delight.
One last thrust,

And you explode.
Our bodies cum in unison.

Now allow your manhood to linger inside,
As my orgasm slowly subsides,
And euphoric waves cause my sugar walls to contract a few
more times.

You can't fight the feelings,
My tunnel of delight is milking the life out of you,
And making love to your soul.

You abruptly push me off in one last attempt to maintain
control,
I laugh out loud,
As I turn and look you in the eyes,
Damn that was one hell of a ride!

<u>Mental Manipulation</u>

Clouds rolling,
Storms roaring,
Thunder cracking,
Lightening flashing,
The perfect scenery for making love.

Aromas of vanilla,
Teddies made of lace and silk,
Satin sheets spread across the bed,
But there's one ingredient missing…
YOU!!!

Your job has pulled you away,
So now,
We must find a creative new way to play.

Your body longs to be touched,
And so does mine,
Tonight,
Allow our minds to stimulate each other,
Causing mental ejaculation all over the sheets.

Tonight,
Facetime will display our sex session,
Skype will bring us face to face,
Allowing both of us to take turns becoming the spectator.

Watch me work my new toy,

Moving and grooving as if it was you.
Watch the passion that your love brings even without you
physically being there,
It feels as if your hands are touching me everywhere.

Now the role is reversed,
Your head leans back,
Envisioning my mouth enveloping you whole,
You sliding in and out,
I'm trying to show Super Head who's the real pro.

We're working in unison,
Each trying to make the other explode,
Lost in pleasure,
Screaming in delight.

You stroke faster,
I pump harder.
With each stroke,
I push deeper,
And with each pump,
You pound relentlessly.

I never knew how mental sex could be,
But I swear it felt like you were inside of me!
Masturbation had never done anything for you,
But this scene was living proof,
That when two people connect spiritually,
Anything is possible.

I can't say that I want to do this on a regular,

But it sure adds spice to our sex life,
And for that I'm glad,

I can't complain,
Cause when it comes to sex,
My man is bad.
And he's happy too,
Because his woman is a sexy, freaky fool!

Grand Announcement

Now comes the sad part… I have truly enjoyed penning this erotic collection but it is now time to say good bye. This was my way of kicking in the doors to the literary world and it definitely did that. I got plenty of shocked faces and awkward looks, especially with the former cover. Yes, I was definitely bold. But I must now evolve as a writer and take on other causes that are dear to my heart and test my boundaries as an author. I want to thank all of you who stood by me, defended me, and rocked with Royal 4 the whole. It will never be forgotten. But be on the lookout because you never know what I just might do. I love you guys deeply and I always will!!!!

-Danielle Bigsby (Formerly Known as Nasti D)

A Little Something Special

Indulge your freaky side and have fun with your mate,
For it is never too late,
Only time awaits.

Try something new,
Cause more freakiness awaits you…

On my radio show:
Raw Sex Uncovered…

Found on W646 Queen City Bullies Radio as of May 29th every Sunday, Monday, and Tuesday night from 11:00 p.m. to Midnight CST!!!

NASTI DESIREZ

www.ingramcontent.com/pod-product-compliance
Lightning Source LLC
Chambersburg PA
CBHW062007040426
42447CB00010B/1955